Finding a Mate: Animal Companions

Cassidy St. James

rourkeeducationalmedia.com

Teaching Focus:
Fluency: Using Expression- Have students read aloud to practice reading with expression and with appropriate pacing.

Before Reading:

Building Academic Vocabulary and Background Knowledge

Before reading a book, it is important to set the stage for your child or student by using pre-reading strategies. This will help them develop their vocabulary, increase their reading comprehension, and make connections across the curriculum.

1. *Read the title and look at the cover. Let's make predictions about what this book will be about.*
2. *Take a picture walk by talking about the pictures/photographs in the book. Implant the vocabulary as you take the picture walk. Be sure to talk about the text features such as headings, Table of Contents, Glossary, bolded words, captions, charts/diagrams, or Index.*
3. Have students read the first page of text with you then have students read the remaining text.
4. *Strategy Talk – use to assist students while reading.*
   - *Get your mouth ready*
   - *Look at the picture*
   - *Think…does it make sense*
   - *Think…does it look right*
   - *Think…does it sound right*
   - *Chunk it – by looking for a part you know*
5. *Read it again.*
6. *After reading the book complete the activities below.*

Content Area Vocabulary
Use glossary words in a sentence.

attracts
call
claim
colony
mate
territory

After Reading:

Comprehension and Extension Activity

After reading the book, work on the following questions with your child or students in order to check their level of reading comprehension and content mastery.

1. *What does courtship mean? (Asking questions)*
2. *What are some ways the animals in the book attracted a mate? (Summarize)*
3. *Why do animals mate? (Summarize)*
4. *How does a peacock attract a mate? (Summarize)*

Extension Activity

Animals are searching for mates that are strong. With a partner, act out ways you would show you are strong and ways to show you are weak. Have your partner guess how you are displaying yourself: strong or weak. Then switch roles with your partner. Discuss how animals show they are strong and why they are able to obtain mates. What happens to animals who are weak?

I like you, do you like me?
Show each other how you feel.

Animal Couples

In the wild, animals must fight for mates. During courtship, animals show that they are strong and healthy.

Lions

Giraffes

The strongest animals will have the strongest babies. Animals **mate** to keep their species alive and strong.

Emperor Penguin

The Emperor Penguin sways as he walks around the **colony**. He lets out a trumpet **call**. When he gets a female's attention, they will stand face-to-face, then bow.

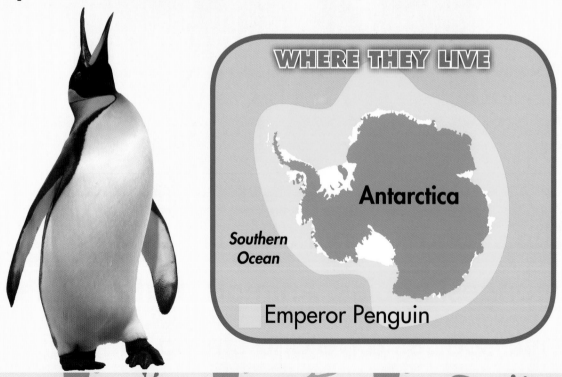

WHERE THEY LIVE

Antarctica

Southern Ocean

Emperor Penguin

The penguin needs a mate. The male sounds strong. His call **attracts** a female.

Emperor Penguins

Both the male and female penguins will care for their egg.

7

Peafowl

The peacock sees a female. He lifts his train of tail feathers. Then he dramatically fans them out, revealing a brilliant display of color.

The peacock needs a mate. The male looks healthy. He attracts a female.

WHERE THEY LIVE

Asia

Africa

Pacific Ocean

Indian Ocean

Peafowl

Peafowl

A peacock is a male and a peahen is a female. Together they are called peafowl.

African Bullfrog

The African bullfrog fills his throat with air. He lets out a loud Crrrroooooaaaak! He is calling for a mate. If he is lucky a female will hear.

WHERE THEY LIVE

Africa

Atlantic Ocean

Indian Ocean

African Bullfrog

The bullfrog needs a mate. The male uses his call to sound strong. He attracts a female.

African Bullfrog

A strong male bullfrog will chase away smaller males.

11

Frigatebird

That bright red chest is sure to turn some heads! The male frigatebird puffs up like a balloon. He wants to impress a female.

Frigatebird

The frigatebird needs to mate. The male looks healthy. His bright chest attracts a female.

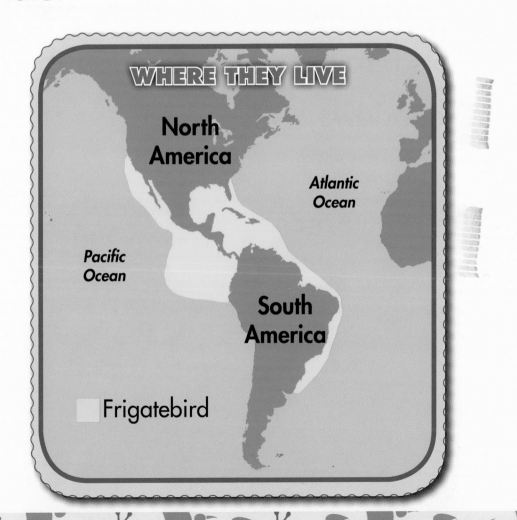

WHERE THEY LIVE

North America

Atlantic Ocean

Pacific Ocean

South America

Frigatebird

Iberian Hare

Hares munch on grasses and flowers. Suddenly, a female hare darts past a male. She lets him chase her through the fields and meadows.

WHERE THEY LIVE

Europe

Atlantic Ocean

Iberian Hare

Africa

The hare needs to mate. The male appears fast and strong. The female picks her mate.

Iberian Hares

Red-Crowned Crane

Bowing, jumping, running, and tossing grass, the red-crowned crane dances for a female. He throws his head back and lets out a loud kar-r-r-o-o-o!

The crane needs to mate. The male dances to show he is strong and healthy. His dance attracts a female.

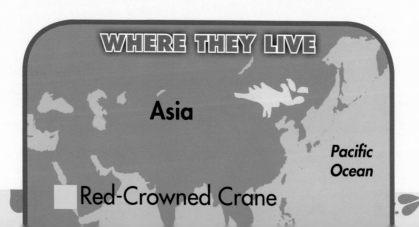

WHERE THEY LIVE

Asia

Pacific Ocean

Red-Crowned Crane

Red-crowned cranes also dance to relieve tension and bond with their mates.

Guanaco

The guanaco looks out for predators while the females eat. His large **territory** has lots of good food.

Guanacos

The guanaco needs to mate. The male makes a safe place. His territory attracts females.

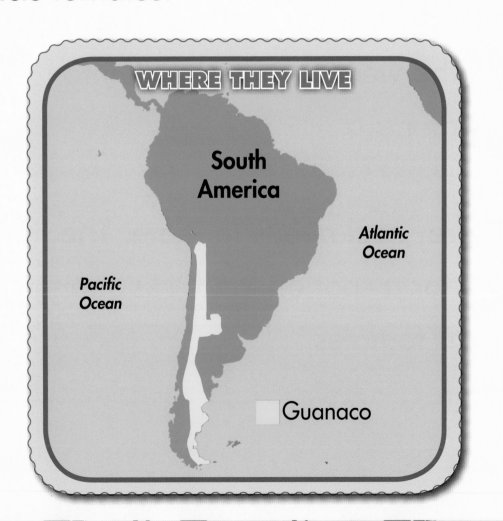

WHERE THEY LIVE

South America

Atlantic Ocean

Pacific Ocean

Guanaco

Grey Seal

Grey seals gather on land. The strong males **claim** their territory. They fight and push the weaker males back into the water.

The grey seal needs to mate. The male fights for a spot on land. His strength attracts females.

When an animal chooses a mate, it's important to find one that is strong and healthy. That way their babies will be healthy and better able to survive in the wild.

WHERE THEY LIVE

North America

Atlantic Ocean

Europe

Grey Seal

Grey Seals

Photo Glossary

attracts (uh-TRAKTS): An animal attracts a mate by getting its attention.

call (kawl): A call is a loud animal sound.

claim (klaym): When you claim something, you say that it belongs to you.

 **colony** (KAH-luh-nee): Animals that live in a colony live with a large group.

 **mate** (mate): A mate is one of a pair of breeding animals.

 **territory** (TER-i-tor-ee): A territory is an area used by a group of animals.

Index

About the Author

Cassidy St. James is the author of numerous books for children and young adults. She enjoys learning about how animals survive in the wild. Cassidy got to see a peacock courtship dance in person while visiting Costa Rica.

Meet The Author!
www.meetREMauthors.com

Websites

www.bbc.co.uk/nature/adaptations/Courtship_display
www.planet-science.com/categories/under-11s/our-world/2011/02/love-in-the-animal-kingdom.aspx
kidscorner.org/html/zoo0206.php

www.rourkeeducationalmedia.com

PHOTO CREDITS: Cover: ©Proframe Photography; title page: olga_gl; page 3: ©JoeLena; page 4: ©Pearl Media; page 5, 11: © Nico Smit; page 6, 22 (middle): ©Kotomiti Okuma; page 7: © BMJ; page 9: ©tezzstock; page 10: ©Am Wu; page 12, 22 (top): ©Stassines; page 15: ©photoL; page 17, 23 (middle): ©plusphoto; page 18, 23 (bottom): ©Pichugin Dmitry; page 21, 22 (bottom): ©AEPhotographic; page 23: ©kkaplin (top)

Edited by: Jill Sherman
Cover design by: Jen Thomas
Interior design by: Rhea Magaro

Library of Congress PCN Data

Finding a Mate: Animal Companions/ Cassidy St. James
(Close Up on Amazing Animals)
ISBN (hard cover)(alk. paper) 978-1-62717-632-3
ISBN (soft cover) 978-1-62717-754-2
ISBN (e-Book) 978-1-62717-875-4
Library of Congress Control Number: 2014934198
Printed in the United States of America, North Mankato, Minnesota

Also Available as:

ROURKE'S
e-Books